Unutterable Blunders and Palace Disasters

Unutterable Blunders and Palace Disasters

Unutterable Blunders
and
Palace Disasters

(Some Published Poems)

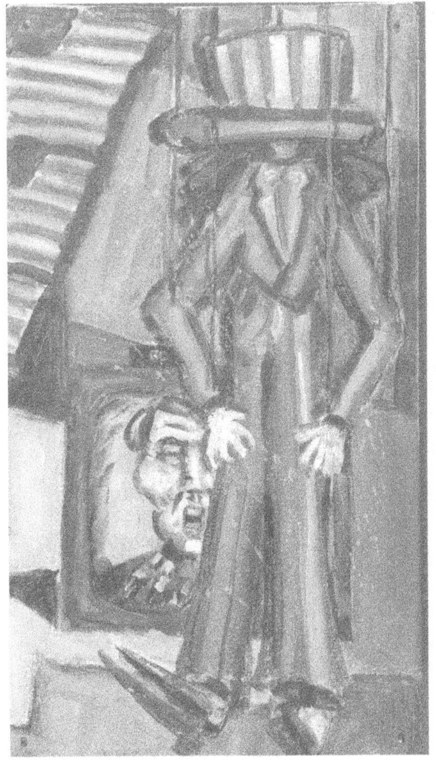

Ken Jones

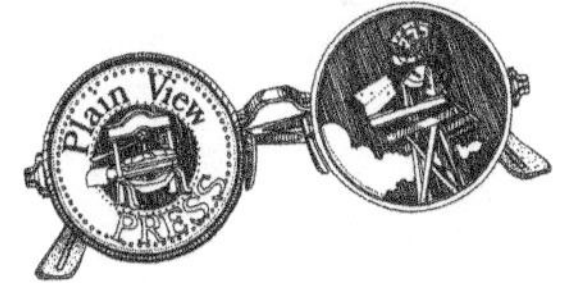

Plain View Press
P. O. 42255
Austin, TX 78704

plainviewpress.net
sbright1@austin.rr.com
512-441-2452
512-440-7139 (fax)

ISBN: 1-891386-57-3
 Library of Congress Number: 2006905231

Cover art by Fletcher Stafford.
Poet Photo by George Reul.
Manuscript typist: Carol Lewis.

Acknowledgements

"Unsolved Mystery" – *Sojourn*, University of Texas at Dallas;
"The Black Earth is Alive with a Riot" – *Lone Stars*, San Antonio,
TX; "Pretensions" – *Patchwork Poems*, San Antonio, TX; "Dizzy"
– *Limestone Circle*, Ashburn, VA; "One Last Shot" – *Patchwork Poems*,
San Antonio, TX; "The Spirit Responds to Pope's 'Essay on Man'"
– *One Dog Press*, Sacramento, CA; "The Old Faithful" – *Spiky Palm*,
Texas A & M, Galveston; "Slices of Middle America" – *Central
Thoughts*, HCC Central, Houston, TX; "Declaration" – *San Fernando
Poetry Journal*, Northridge, CA; "Song of Myself or The Materialist
Manifesto" – *Mojo Risin'*, Chicago, IL; "Legal Tender" – *Vol. No.*,
Newhall, CA; "Mid-Wilshire Sunset" – *Freedom isn't Free*, Orange,
CA / *Mojo Risin'*, Chicago, IL; "Volcano" – *Black Cross*, Long Beach,
CA; "Quaker Oats" – *FIZ*, Los Angeles, CA; "Certainty" – *Yawp!*, Los
Angeles, CA; "Prophecy" – *Thee Neverending Page*, Huntington Beach,
CA; "I Slay Me" – *Concho River Review*, Angelo State University, TX;
"The Thracian Maid: Updated" – *Patchwork Poems*, San Antonio, TX;
"Lies Beyond the Why" – *Lone Stars*, San Antonio, TX; "The Great
Chain" – *MAP of Austin Poetry*, Austin TX / *Patchwork Poems*, San
Antonio, TX; "The Chain" – *San Fernando Poetry Journal*, Northridge,
CA; "The Condemned Complex" – *Freedom isn't Free*, Orange, CA;
"Planless Mass" – *Patchwork Poems*, San Antonio, TX; "Willingly
Browbeat" – *In Our Own Words, Vol. 3*, Raleigh, NC / *San Fernando
Poetry Journal*, Northridge, CA; "Half-Off" – *Lone Stars*, San Antonio,
TX; "Papua Paradigm" – *Patchwork Poems*, San Antonio, TX; "What
in the World Leads Life" – *Patchwork Poems*, San Antonio, TX;
"Earth Becomes the World" – *TimeSlice*, Houston, TX; "The Sun
Transcends the Scene" - *One Dog Press*, Davis, CA; "Still Life: Venice
Beach Workers" – *Saturday Afternoon Journal*, Los Angeles, CA; "East
Side Amble" – *Lean Seed, San Jacinto College*, South, Houston, TX;
"The Pilgrim" – *NaCL*, Clear Lake, TX, "Square Dance" – *Midtown
Magazine* (online), Houston, TX; "Missing" – *Flying Horse*, Austin,
TX; "Doubting Words" -*Flying Horse*, Austin, TX; "Begone Godmen!"
–*Vision Quest*, Austin, TX; "Swift's Scatalogical Shit" – *Flying Horse*,
Austin, TX; "The Continuing Saga of Signior Dildo" – *Flying Horse*,
Austin, TX; "69" – *Midtown Magazine*, Houston, TX and *LegaMedia.net*
(German website); "Know that Evil is Close at Hand" – *Poetry Super*

Highway (online); "Tongue Tied" – *Freedom isn't Free*, Orange, CA; "By the Light of the T.V. Set" – *San Fernando Poetry Journal*, Northridge, CA; "The Supermarket" – *San Fernando Poetry Journal*, Northridge, CA; "Bliss Paralysis" – *HIP 3*, Houston, TX; "Life Studies in Four Chapels" – *Diverse City*, Austin, TX; "The Totem Pole" – *San Fernando Poetry Journal*, Northridge, CA; "Calling a Spade a Spade" – *Zillah*, Port Aransas, TX; "The Camp Psychologist" – *Saturday Afternoon Journal*, Los Angeles, CA; "Braciaca" – *Twilight Ending*, Milford, CT; "What Windows This?" – *Tributaries*, Dalton College, GA; "And All That" – *One Dog Press*, Davis, CA; "The Car Wreck" – *Parnassus Literary Journal*, Forest Park, GA; "Old Man Ode" – *Diverse City*, Austin, TX; "It's a Small World, After All" – *Reflect*, Norfolk, VA; "Noose" – *Patch Poems*, San Antonio, TX; "Unutterable Blunders and Palace Disasters" – *San Fernando Poetry Journal*, Northridge, CA.

Apologies for any errors or omissions.

Introduction

While compiling this collection, I had two main criteria in mind. One was to only include published poems. Poets are by nature solitary solipsists and extreme egomaniacs. My theory is that if an editor found the piece good enough to publish, it must have some extrinsic worth. The second criterion was to provide some sense of my philosophy of life. My poetry is in a sense a personal cosmology. I am not a huge fan of the modern workshop, where the self-contained image is exalted above all. I wanted this collection to reflect a certain socio-political viewpoint (mine) in all its cynical, hopeful, reductionist, expansionist, dystopian and utopian complexity. Hopefully the reader will gain a little enjoyment and enlightenment from these pieces.

Ken Jones
Houston, TX
2006

There is no opportunity for revolution in America…
America is essentially a country of pious peasants

Bertrand Russell

Contents

Introduction 7
Unsolved Mystery 13
The Black Earth Is Alive With a Riot 14
Pretensions 15
Dizzy 16
One Last Shot 17
The Spirit Responds To Pope's "Essay on Man" 18
The Old Faithful 19
Slices Of Middle America 20
Declaration 21
Song Of Myself Or the Materialist Manifesto 22
Legal Tender 23
Mid-Wilshire Sunset 25
Volcano 26
Quaker Oats 27
The Supermarket 28
Certainty 29
Prophecy 30
I Slay Me 31
The Thracian Maid: Updated 32
Lies Beyond the Why 33
The Great Chain 34
The Chain 35
The Condemned Complex 36
Planless Mass 37
Willingly Browbeat 38
Half-Off 39
Papua Paradigm 40
What In the World Leads Life 41
Earth Becomes the World 42
The Sun Transcends the Scene 43
Still Life: Venice Beach Workers 44
East Side Amble 45
The Pilgrim 46
Square Dance 47
Missing 48
Doubting Words 49
Begone, Godmen! 50
Swift's Scatalogical Shit 51
The Continuing Saga Of Signior Dildo 52

69   54
Know That Evil Is Close At Hand   55
Tongue Tied   56
The Totem Pole   57
By the Light Of the T.V. Set   58
Bliss Paralysis   59
Life Studies In Four Chapels   60
Calling a Spade a Spade   61
The Camp Psychologist   62
Braciaca *   63
What Windows This?   64
And All That   65
The Car Wreck   66
Old Man Ode   67
It's a Small World, After All   68
Noose   69
Unutterable Blunders and Palace Disasters   70
About the Author   73

Unsolved Mystery

History: the mystery of a monkey's mastery
Over a dirt speck flecked with organic strands
Linked ladders pissing bladders full
Of animate animals born to degenerate.
There is a key: It's easy.
But stinky red herrings throw us
Off the hunt's scent.
Our heads bent down, sniffing ground
Trod and retrod into sod and God
Knows what else how often.
What's in the skull dulls in the effort,
Cracks against a rock hard wall
But in mongoloid monotony keeps jerking
Still smashing against the wall.
No benevolent omniscient doctor around
To force us to wear a helmet.
So jerk and smash, jerk and dull thud
Duller, duller. The pull of the push to smash.
Like gazing in a fireplace entrances
As the stack cackles and the flame
Exclaims a warm glow
That scalds on contact.
The real mystery is the continuous
How and why, coterminous

The Black Earth Is Alive With a Riot

(for E.O. Wilson)

In every iota of ancient biota
The sheer veneer of life spirit
Mistress Earth wears, tears.
Discordant hordes of howler
Monkeys–name of sapiens –
Rape the harmony. Pierce the silence
Of dense diverse universes–myopic
To Apocalypse till it slips its
Kill tool in our skull.
In the crannied wall the miracle flower
Devours its essence – a firefly hungry
To eat its mate in one final meal
Before the lethal injection.
I know spirit and sapiens –
Which will rule? Which teaches?
Which warning siren will we
Snore through or ignore?
She is angry – she has every right
To wish to spit us back to void.
To cancel this damsel in distress
Is our destiny. Its history. It ain't pretty.

Pretensions

We lived in the wild, picking
   berries from trees.
Plunging fingers
   into the dirt for roots.
For meat, we beat
   small animals to death,
   wrapped their uncooked flesh
   in dried leaves placed
   over a fire of sticks
Collected by day
To protect us at night.

Around this flaming focus
We spoke of the day's events.
Men told of the land
   vast as the darkness,
   teeming with creatures.
Women listened in silence,
   tending the children.

For warmth, we wrapped our arms
   around each other
   and huddled.
We gazed into space before sleep
Wondering
   what was there
   that wasn't here.
The wilderness
   undressed our pretensions.

Dizzy

Getting dizzy is
The Original buzz.
Children turn circles
Not futile but full
Of discovery – the love
Of leaving the unchanging
Way things are for
New precipices of perception.
The height is, well,
Dizzying, that first night
They spin and grin
And hit the carpet,
The same dumb numb normalcy
Crumbles in that tumble,
Then they do it again
And again – the faster the better
The ceiling starts swirling
The room's not the same
Room they spun in
Before. The floor
Feels fluid. The furniture
Flies by in swarms of brown.
The fall is coming
And welcome. They lie back
And watch this different world
Race at their eyes.
Their smile lingers long after
Their head clears. Reality deals
Damn nice hands sometimes.

One Last Shot

To heal the Earth we must first heal ourselves
Of impurities we surely imbibed
At the shot bar of More Progress and Wealth.

We clean the bottles off the dusty shelves
To make way for the New Age we've described.
To heal the Earth we must first heal ourselves

And then never again dirty our wells:
Those storehouses needed for all the tribes
At the shot bar of More Progress and Wealth.

Unavoidable poisons, with shrewd stealth
Have stolen in with suicidal bribes.
To heal the Earth we must first heal ourselves

And learn the subtle cycle for her health.
She's not the whore our self-hate did proscribe
At the shot bar of More Progress and Wealth.

She is our source, our fountain whose vibe
Gives us the life on which we now inscribe:
To heal the Earth we must first heal ourselves
At the shot bar of More Progress and Wealth.

The Spirit Responds To Pope's "Essay on Man"

Lo, the rich Caucasian? whose disciplined mind
Misses the Goddess in the sky, deaf to her spirit in the wind.
A soulless husk. Science and Hubris teach him to stray
Through theories of galaxies or the Sun's torchéd way;
His civilization strips hope from his person
Crowded cloud shrouded hills – his prison
Some pristine niche in clean rooms embraced
Some antiseptic directive in the solid waste.
Masters of mother country – they behold
The last dying hours, counting its gold.
Always questioning natural desire
He finds guardians in the all within
And the without, in wide horizon sky
He trashes just for the Company.

The Old Faithful

To you ancient mighty geyser
I flow in exploding ecstasy
The bubbling Bacchus passion
Shoots through you to breathing me
My soul: the mental invention
Of ancestors wrestling questions
Of endless insignificance, stretches
As far back as cuneiform scratches
This mystic intoxication instead
Clots and stops the words I bleed
Into a cracked back splattered head
A conspiracy theory of human history.
As if history explained anything
Except the surface bubbles carving sadness
On the endless unlike faces
Their hot tears simmer in memory
And blossom in pressure passion.

Slices Of Middle America

Doll cottages dot the dark tar boulevards
Glowing "home" for some animate animal
A temple of temperate comfort
And fixed feeding time
In a frenzy of pituitary culinary
With his chosen monogamous mate
Who faithfully holds down the homestead
As he battles the elements for survival
They are not strangers.
Their ancestors conquered the virgin land
Fled famine for freedom, tamed
The Plains buffalo, hid
The misnomered natives
Who ferried across the Bering Strait
As slope nose Oriental anthropoids
The original Amerasians.
"Much deeper and you'll hit China!"
The grizzled prospector yells
At the spike driving coolie
Not thinking a gold Caddie
Awaits his descendants down the track
When they open a dining car
On stationary Chinatown plot
And net two million per annum
Feeding pink-skinned tourists
Who claim it as their special spot
"Our home away from home"

Declaration

When in the cycle of existence, A Time arises when

All Peoples; despite nationality, despite ethnicity,
   despite the desperate dance all waltz

Come together in Defiance of the Former Order
   –   To halt the faulty industry; its Creation devoured in
           Waste
   –   To repair the raped ecosystem; the Goddess in her
           Rightful Place
   –   To heal the Whole Social Covenant; From Hunger to trust in
           Government
   –   To embrace change: fundamental, difficult, yet
           needed now;

   And reanimate the Life Spirit after our experiment in
           restless senselessness

We used to embrace these truths: Now it's self evident
that while all humans are individuals, this fact kills our
will to hold true liberty as mates.

We are all endowed with the presence of the Life Essence.
We must journey froth Together to form in our souls
One World, with Liberty and Justice for All.

Song Of Myself Or the Materialist Manifesto

I want a mansion
With a million fancy gadgets
To service my every wanton whim.
A chauffer-driven limousine
With chocolate boxes and Mr. Boston bottles
Strewn like bones in the back.
Where I can skin an animal
For printed pieces of paper
And clothe my homebound mate.
Or I can play Icarus
And jet to Greece
To wallow in olive oil
With sun-worshipping nudes.
To tread the Parthenon steps
And maybe to spit.
I'm proud to be an American.
The "new Darwinism"
Finds no fault with me.
Gold incisored materialism
Is not amorality
It's just facing reality.
We were born into the jackpot
Why apologize
Or plunge into downwardly mobile asceticism.
"But your soul, son
Your soul will go hungry."
Well, I feed on greed
That All-American
Fortified corn meal
Artificially sweetened to taste
Just right for me.
Call me Faust
And I'll buy you a beer.

Legal Tender

Their eyes chisel guilt into my skull.
Brigade after brigade in rumpled unkempt swarms
Lean in lines outside store windows
Their faces a woven mat of misery.
From this distance, my pity
Fears to focus on a single visage
Afraid my shame will surge in red waves
Across the stone countenance I maintain
In my mid-day stroll down Los Angeles Street.
In jewelry store foyers and bank lobbies
Stand guards ominously perched
If only I was merchandise
A product with a measurable price
A gold chain or diamond pendant
Something they could defend
Without reprimand.
At Grand I duck inside a bar
Order a vodka soda, then slam a shot of tequila
To feel
To my right a man wears his forty years as sixty
Sees my gaze shift to him
And offers to buy me a round. I readily agree
Any bonding in this human hell is sacred.
He tells his tale: military service, divorce, the bus
That at midnight will return him home to Oklahoma,
The thick wad of dollars in a wallet
Stacked like a bulletproof vest in his chest pocket,
And a scar from barroom brawls:
He shows his stomach. Too polite to stare I smile weakly
But he insists I touch it.
My finger reaches to feel its length
Snaking his torso like a rake on a chalkboard
But at the last moment I flinch
Crack my weak defeated smile

continued

And walk out without a thank you.
Back to the street again and two men
Beg for nickels – praying the trickle down
Theory operates in my fat face
It does. But tears aren't exactly easily convertible
Legal tender.

Mid-Wilshire Sunset

A pollutant palette splatters cosmetic pink
Across an artificially eerie L.A. sunset.
Brightness leaps to life
Like an Impressionist canvas –
A Vuillard with blank-faced women
Taking tea in a parlor of flowers.
It neither knows nor cares,
or is screaming a warning.
We apply the make-up to those faces
In our ignitions and exhausts.
Other colors fight for space:
Monoxide mauve, chemical chartreuse.
Like drivers in a mad dash for the on-ramp,
What's left of the pure clear sky
Fades away in perspective, like the baby
Used as a beggar's tool
By a runaway camped at a convenience store –
Both casualties of capricious cruelty.
Gone mad but making sense.

Volcano

We wear our fears in our eyes
Like anchors dropped in oceans –
Currents of senses and emotions
In furious churning yearning
To break the banal bonds
Which bind our minds in dying bodies.
And your beauty is an island newly formed
From the Earth hotly urging
Dominance by purging
Its menstruous in a senseless
Replication of creation.
So to feel our bodies
Shake in exultation at our union
Buries these fears in layers
Of ecstatic islands mindlessly rising.

Quaker Oats

Lumpy baby sputum?
Seagull feces?
Elephant ejaculate?
No! – bland powder mixed with water
Not clam chowder or baked beans
But a grueling taste test.
The secular American housewife
Who chimes orgasmic release
Like clockwork, once a week,
Buys a cardboard cylinder
A pre-packaged meal
For her ungrateful,
Sensation-satiated babies
Whose faces curdle as they cuddle
Warm bowls in tiny hands
Thinking, "An angry God
Must have made this stuff."

The Supermarket

A dream! A dream!
Gleaming, streaming
Freedom, screaming
Needs fulfilled and killed
By steaming steel.
The tattletale rat-a-tat of jackhammers
Don't drill here.
Mechanical musical tones
Ooze soothing tongues
Of acoustic and psychic manipulation.
No more forest foraging for you!
These aisles smile
Wink wishes
Radiate amazing wealth
And ionize apathy.
The sterile decay of a dumbwaiter
Locked in the service closet.

Certainty

Certainty is knowing nothing
Children find frightening is funny.
Their fear is a miniature
Of familiar details
They can't add up
To a larger picture.
A child cuts his finger
And sucks it –
Food and blood are brothers.
A child stares into darkness
And sees nothing certain.

Prophecy

I admire intensity
The quest for cerebral celebrity
Feeding rumbling hungers
Of understandable origin.
The fuse that drove his flowing
To a time-lapse picture burn-out,
The lens of poetic resolution
Lost in too-clear focusing.
Another Welshman dead from drink.

My ancestry is also Welsh.
My father's father,
Who I never knew,
Cut rock
To make his mark,
Mount his buck.
He made cornerstones.
Poured foundations
He could never know
Would survive in
Umbilically tied
Memories
Of an unknown grandson
Who constructs skyscrapers of syllables
Catwalking between a restful balance,
An overarching acceptance;
Or a vile repulsion
That words and stone
And these electric mental impulses
Are cut from the same quarry.

I Slay Me

"Scratch the surface," she said, "and you'll find that underneath it's
solid Red Bank."

Eileen Simpson, Poets in Their Youth, p. 182

Suicidal, homicidal
Dispossessed, depressed
Poets in their youth dispute
To root out their best.
Half starved, laughs carved
In false face facades
Versifiers vent steamed spleens
Rules of verse disbarred.
Verisimilitude, attitude
Narrow brows and brood
Bile of internal exiles
The rickety artists' food
Art parched, pen starched
Rumpled shirts in unkempt swarms
Warmed by ignored tomes
Gloating over unread harms.

The Thracian Maid: Updated

The stargazer fell into a deep pool.
His housekeeper had to laugh.
"Oh, so you joke at your master's expense,"
he bellowed, "Feed on his wheat,
forget whose chaff you separate,
on whose staff your life depends,
the simple ends and means of your days;
while I ask of the sky…why?"

"I can't say I'm truly sorry, sir,"
in a weary warble, the maid replied.
"It's just…you're such a strange creature
your weird words are never in my world.
Among the babble in the malls
or voices in offices, no one ever cries
Why? Why not nothing?!
The people in my husband's company…"

"Are mere vendors of necessities!"
the astral asker barked back rather harshly,
then thought better;
"I don't mean less worthy or somehow inferior.
Yet when I wonder at the dome of the interior,
at what's beyond, or even why we know what's here,
the shock rocks me back, my balance disturbed,
So, of course, I often fall backwards."

"But you know the pool will catch you," she objected.
And he was struck dumb by her wisdom.

Lies Beyond the Why

We surrendered time
To the Renaissance realm
A trope of the sublime
Drives wild at the helm.
We abdicated space
At the century's gates
No place the only place
Dwell the subatomic Fates.
As one Earth expires
The random hand weaves
Dark quark quagmires
Protozoan tea leaves.
Cantankerous carbon
Elemental material
Live from dead, some from none
Mirrors the visible.
The fall of an apple
Shocks electromagnetic
Weak and strong holds on particles
Keep Cosmos copasetic.
A desire to unify
Forces beyond the eye
Whole horizon and sky
Lies beyond the why.

The Great Chain

Great Chain of Being! You have connected
The walls and windows where I lie protected
Hives where wasps wonder what's what
Cicadas who shiver in leaves' pleasure huts

Nests of stalks and discarded candy wrappers
Built by the homebirds in suburban rafters
Thin, tinny chirps of two baby swallows
Whose open mouths cry out, hungry and shallow

Voices of wandering children, uttering "Where?"
As adults answer back, muttering "Why?"
Squeals of doors opening to forgotten universes
Hidden empty pockets in a socialite's purse

Chinaberries clustered heroically atop
Gently swaying branches whose life never stops
Chimes from ornate clocks of precise manufacture
Priests seeking absolution in a barren prefecture

Then back to these scratchings, my breath exhales
My plastic souvenir pen and roiling entrails
Great Chain – take me beyond this latest veil
I am a child before your sea – now fill my pail.

The Chain

Where will the chain of capital next lead?
Into chips that slip into disks of knowledge storage?
Into receptacles for chemicals whose residue pollutes?
Into new-fueled carriages to move us from origin to carrion?
Into constructs to entertain, meant to forget our burden?
Or like a self-consumptive servant back into itself
Will capital flow like a channel into a stagnant reservoir
Filling the banks with the guiltless silt of numbers' labor
Into the summer cottages and winter retreats
Into the pudgy fingers and silken palms
Of clean condo-dwelling beings
Who know no more about its creation or dissipation than
We know about the universe: that it is there and
We are here and we use it and live in its all-consuming shadow
But feel the emptiness at its core
And scream to escape the chain we can't explain or break.

The Condemned Complex

This building, my hands
Aimed to etch, came to watch
My sensations dissipate,
My will to feel stolen.
These walls were my canvas.
The lumps and air bubbles – my refracted reflection.
The distraction of asphyxiation
Never bothered me. I breathed
A rarefied air of inability anyway.
I overheard the jostling molecules
Mocking Michelangelo, talking of me
Screaming in silent synesthesia
My apologia for existing.
While the skeletal easel melted
Into this witches brew
Of feelings I vomit
And in gagging on, renew.

Planless Mass

What's the matter
is matter:
its seemingly
endless patterns,
configurations
predicated on atoms
smashing at random.
Our single spaced
existence veils
this Chaos face.
So only when
our "soul's"
power plant
generates sustenance,
hence…waste,
does Homo Americanus,
that high-falutin'
proof of evolution,
face that face
he hates
yet so longs
to embrace.
His master and creator
Nature
all cut-throat and Planless.

Willingly Browbeat

If no morals are good for the morale,
a generation of cheerleaders, saints,
and party martyrs can't possibly fail.
My peers proudly display taint and war paint
from battles with the bottle and condoms.
An OD of unearned prosperity
has rendered them numb, subservient, dumb –
its origin to them a mystery.
Why paper mediates labor, transfers
Flop sweat into products, then exchanges
ultimate worth for essential numbers –
the whole work's cancer, self-eating, deranged.
Where too-sure comfort's passion's defeat,
why not genuflect, willingly browbeat?

Half-Off

Brooks Brothers announces a special sale
For a limited time only – your life –
Bind yourself in our fine cut cloth, grow pale.
Take a docile and subservient wife.
Drive to glass or concrete towers each day
Stain dead tree with ink as computer chips
Tally commodity transfers – your pay –
Then off through electric lit night you slip
To Happy Hour where seven whiskey sours
Paint a faint grin over your clown grimace.
Hollow echoes mock your outward power
Tail snapped in the trap, twitch in this race
Daily lies mercifully few in number
Till dignity is a blank mirror stare.

Papua Paradigm

To act civilized down in New Guinea
Means bones in the nose and heads on a stick
Women and pigs are equally pretty
Such dumb docility is quite a trick.
From Port Moresby fly the wise curious
To witness this slice of Man's history
How the genteel view this as spurious
Is surely the far greater mystery.
Tribes warring for the sheer joy of killing
Blood paint, skin and hide clothing and penis sheaths
Primates yank life from Nature unwilling
To grant importance to their life or death.
So a toast to the headhunter's valley
Here humans live as themselves, truly free.

What In the World Leads Life

What in the world leads life
Around on an energy chain – it is
The East and Juliet is the moon.
On a carved lowered window
I lean to examine diverse universes.
Insistent, their resilience
Shines brilliantly in the Western sky.
The Dog Star point toward one
Milky Way not stamped with

The Universal Product Code. Who
Deciphers these vertical lines –
Computer owners or pudgy, grease stained
Laborers lappin' up the spilled milk.
The puddled come muddling along
Dirty in the shared fecal stream.
She carries kisses in the consciousness
Of the wind and inanimate objects answering.

Earth Becomes the World

Pangea! Pangea!
Pithecine precursor,
Original continental mass.
Eons of erosion
On Oceania's floor
Broke the crustal plates.
The food didn't spill.
The teeming, steaming
Organic ferment
Churned and burned
On each fragment,
Exploding in cornucopias
Of symbiotic sister species,
Animate animals adapting
Nucleotides to niche.
The scene grew
Nearly indecipherable.
The screen swirled
With masses of adaptations.
Earth became the World
To those pithecines
Who filled the screen
Became its control console
Crammed the picture with demands –
Details their mental
Advancement imposed on
Its directionless direction
Meaning milked from snow.

The Sun Transcends the Scene

Envision plains as open
As the mouth of a milk carton
In every gulp lies latent carrion
Blossoming like dandelions on green
Hard acid-laced asphalt.

Still Life: Venice Beach Workers

She filmed the workers working
But they weren't happy to see her.
The grass still set in concrete
Waiting for the brooms to swoop through.
Meanwhile, her cinematographer dickered.
He needed a lens change.
She told him to stare at the workers
Shoveling gravel into a wheelbarrow
He said, "The bright orange suits are cute
But reflect too much light."
"Just get the shots," she shouted.
"Looks like that one's rising a might."
And one man raised his arm to his brow
To wipe away the sweat. But the rest
Just stood and looked pissed. Not quite ready
To rise.

East Side Amble

I walk through a street of adobe
Where nobody knows me
Men in tattered black
Strewn like empty spray paint cans
Flat on their back
Smile at me as a fellow traveler.
The barbed wire piled high
Glistens like a diamond mine
Atop the liquor stores and boarded shops
Where the great green wheel never stops.
Inside
Brown eyes flat as a desert mesa
Hold their own beauty
In dignity strangely silent yet screaming.

The Pilgrim

(inspired by the statue in the Cullen Sculpture Garden)

Standing half-naked before the world
He enters a new land on spindly legs
Of a mount half-beaten by the task.
Hardly silent upon a peak in Darien
But mouth shut tight at what rough fate awaits.

His fragile, vacant form speaks gigabytes.
His bald head and bulging eyes – affright with light
Like a Roswell alien. He clutches the reins
Of a stout horse whose chest –
Like an empty billboard across the Interstate –
Lies blank with the promise of the next step.

Both their heads point left toward
A Right to a future unencumbered by this tension.
Tomorrow, when they arrive at that land they intent upon,
A faint light will penetrate their eyes
And both will rest. In another worn-out country
Another horse and rider await the next trek.

Square Dance

Picture the traditional American square dance
And brainwashed children chanting
Jewish scriptures and German war tunes
Arm-in-arm – History's hog calling
Promenade and do-si-do – Swing your partner
Round and round – now reverse
Whatever progress you have made,
A bluejean dress and tablecloth skirt
Look tight on your teacher in the corner
Where she claps – Happy this history
Lives and breathes the chants of children
Turning circles inside squares reenacting
The traditional American square dance.

Missing

Missing children
On my milk
Smiled for snapshots
Cardboard portraits
Did they suck
Nourishing nipples
Or choke on force fed
Fecal material
Did some run
From their home
On purpose
To escape
Daddy's furrowed brow and belt
Buckle – he chuckles
Burps bourbon and raises
His steel-tipped snake
Again to the head
Of this third-grade face
On the left of the carton –
Did the boy on the right,
Bobby Joe Barton,
Bring a smile
To a pedophile
As his little Levis tore?
I'll never know
So back in the fridge
They go.

Doubting Words

Life begins when you doubt everything that came before you
— Karl Marx

And so I doubt. I doubt
The proletarian paradise –
Dull hominids unite!
Cast off strife, though strife
Be Nature's way to say
There seems to be
Violence in this universe
Of much beauty
And delicate elegance.
Your busy Industry
Much like bugs and other
Land adapted
Bundles of cells,
Conquered King Nature
And wedded Queen Comfort
When one less dull
Culled and tilled
The brown stuff. Made the green stuff
Reproduce – you too grew –
Grew to reproduce,
Fight for life
Then win and turn the fight
Inwards – and words
Are part and parcel of the violence.
My brain can't sustain
The weight of paradise's paradox.

Begone, Godmen!

You whose tunes
Of funeral ruins wreck
Yellow jelly gullibles.
Inject numbing narcotics
Between the pages of pain
Solemnly declared as law.
On my knees I don't believe
The carpet burns spring from hell.
My downcast eyes examine
Plastic generic Saltines
Body of Christ; wine is blood.
My empty-brained home remains
As true as ever; I do
Too have compassion for all
The experimental rats
Given a huge overdose
Of question-stunting pablum
A pacifier like I
Sucked for security 'til
At nine I birthed a mind,
What bitter taste do I now choose?
The Wager placed – I lose.

Swift's Scatalogical Shit

Jonathan, on a pot I sit
So unlike an ancient dirt pit
Tile gleams its artificial smile
Plumbing removes the putrid pile
Once I, for fun (to understand
What movements guided your Swift hand)
Squatted above a newspaper
Let "Births and Deaths" sniff my vapors
The blessing of solid substance
Dangling in its ritual dance
Hit the "Weddings and Engagements"–
I felt your presence in the scent.
Then into the plumbing I dumped
The odious offal with lumps
Wondered what question next to address
Then saw my lover's empty dress.
Jonathan, you must accept Fate
Women do feel the press of waste
The uncomfortable look of stress
Objects stuck to anal tresses
The sadness of noxious gasses
The gladness when they come to pass.
But such facts emit no reason
To hate not nature, but women.
Doomed hominids are all we are
You've stripped this fact completely bare
So, Dearest Dean Swift, never fear
Brown stains will always slash white underwear.

The Continuing Saga Of Signior Dildo

– to John Wilmot, Earl of Rochester, this verse is humbly dedicated

Animals in the act of creation
Gather in bathtubs with lathered, smooth skin
But four hundred years of history show
No beast pleasures flesh like SIGNIOR DILDO.

Once a fop of Corinthian leather
Now, hard, spiked plastic and only better
He wears every color of the rainbow –
Technology salutes SIGNIOR DILDO.

When you visit hardcore porno bookstores
Behind the counter lie delights galore
Nitrous oxide, XXX videos
And, of course, our hero SIGNIOR DILDO.

Down the street in the Greek habitations
Frat boys discover "Greek's" connotations
Moans rise like flies from Sorority Row
Vocals courtesy of SIGNIOR DILDO.

You women of Austin, shed your sick tricks
Of deceiving rabid men's stiffened pricks
By now you should know the right place to go
The loving, plastic glans of SIGNIOR DILDO.

While in private with your newly-found friend
Discover the fun of good vibrations
Batteries included means, well, you know,
Many a wild ride on SIGNIOR DILDO.

Don't fear that this stud will ever leave town
But do shed a tear 'cause he can't go down
No fun tongueing while you watch his length grow
Ah, the price you pay for SIGNIOR DILDO.

His charms, scarce addressed in public discourse
Hope to reach the world through this humble verse
Recited on T.V. or radio
Even the airwaves praise SIGNIOR DILDO.

Now I fear my rhyme has come to a close
But next week I promise more episodes
Tune in for another exciting show
Of the continuing saga of SIGNIOR DILDO.

I'd love to make love to Emily Dickinson
Share Muse, symbiotic sensuality.
Throw poems like roses
Over our shoulders
As we tumbled in summer
Petals and pollen. What passion!
What physical poetry we could
Pour before and into each other.
Fighting the frightening World
With our Wobbling words
Fresh from the press
I could preach my sermons
On the random and she could sing
Her Protesting hymns
to me in only slightly
off-rhythm. We could both
Begin to understand each other.

Know That Evil Is Close At Hand

One fly buzzes us
In Mauthausen's gas chamber
So many spirits.

Tongue Tied

My tongue is tied into tails
Gordian knots that never fail
A fighter-bomber jet-fume trail
Trails into the atmosphere.
I pray before the satin altar
Wine flows from a silver canister
I inhale frankincense, myrrh
My actions stem from fear.

The Totem Pole

"Squat on that!" he spat
And I, intrinsically respectful
Of any societal symbol
Spat back, "You belligerent brat!
Wrap the totemic faces
In ladder-like strands
Around your mental center
Of reverence. Don't you ever
Defile this temple's steeple again:
the Super Glue
Of tribal instinct,
The plumed Panopticon
Feeding the animate fires
The hunters gather around
The T.V. antennae
I refuse to sit on.

By the Light Of the T.V. Set

I write by the light
Of the T.V. set.
I get different hues
With the change on the news
Channel from fight shots
To war pictures.
Both bathe red
Easily accessible light
By which for me to write
On my paper, but later
Both kaleidoscope up the spectrum
Illuminating the stuck periscope
My thoughts become trapped through
When I try to capture them.
Their murky incompleteness even through
525 lines of resolution
Make me more resolute
A hopeful revolution
Can spawn a new human
Cooperation, a plan
Untried not tied to
Inaccurate inanities,
Immaculate insanity.
So I need to write
By the light of the T.V. set
Some more.

Bliss Paralysis

"I exist" I hissed
As an indifferent mist
Filled my words, my artifice
My battle with the abyss

Though loathed and devoid
Of any obvious need to join
A compendium of worrisome scrums
I still tackle understanding it All

I'm immature, impure
I'm manure on the furniture
Skewered by a demure, fatuous persona
Studious to strenuous bejabber

I'm addled by laughter
Stained by a claim of raiment
Debauched, graying,
And slowly dying.

Life Studies In Four Chapels

The Cathedral in your heart holds many chapels.
The first: a tomb from home
Past bad habits cross the cupola's dome
A marble sarcophagi where your dreams lie
Frescoes of fright line the walls
You pray you'll never return to that stall.

At the apse a chapel donated by the wealth
Wasted in your youth. The walls, bare and empty,
Unpainted but tainted
By all that promise washed away.

The central altarpiece displays a crucified Christ
Your self-portrait, clamped in a vise
A triptych of today's achievement:
One panel: lost hope's bereavement
The middle depicts your sickness
Wan, pallid, hopeless.
The third: a hurried, blurred present
Forgotten importance lines the descent.

Finally, in some forgotten corner,
The light from a sacramental candle:
A reminder of why you left home to pray
Of the dissipated youth where you played
Of the stigmata of your artificial sacrifice
And a reason to keep the flame burning bright.

Calling a Spade a Spade

Shovel History's dirt
Upon the intolerant consciousness of Ignorance.
Tunnel into a new tomorrow
Beyond antiquated sorrow.

We are creatures of accreted perceptions
Fossilized into a sedimentary layer
Of human hells, molds we have been told
Must hold us eternally (or for a moment).

But we are really free creatures
No matter ethnicity, the accident
Of residence or birth, the fresh dirt
Piled upon that grave – This freedom saves
This freedom saves!

The Camp Psychologist

You know an enlightened spirit when you see one –
No chance callous remarks
Emerge from its form
When the inevitable dark
Urges the person toward harm –
A depth of spirit leads a golden rule to Truth and Sun.

Wisdom is a difficult attribute to define
But actions speak volumes
And reactions encode CD encyclopedias.
In a fin-de-siecle American room –
Learn tolerance from available media
Daily reruns till the end of time –
Might! Make that spirit shine!

We can reach Buddahood – believe it exists
Two cents appear at your feet
Trying to replay your strong sense
Of what this society needs to meet
Further words from the pauper prince
Until the still stark shills cease to resist.

Braciaca *

Braciaca waits in the grass by the ruins
  her Goddess song is always in tune
Seaweed hair dyed gold as the sunrise
She drifts in the waves with smiles miles wide.

Braciaca counts the stones in a circle
  her Holy voice kisses the breeze still
Dolphin skin smooth as the new fallen rain
She laps up the laughter and stands whole again.

She is the Goddess whose touch moves the wind
She is the spirit our Earth seeks to find.

Braciaca blesses this glade with her fragrance
  Crosses this forest in a pagan dance
Naked breasts glimmer in shimmering twilight
Braciaca's soul never gives up the fight.

* The Celtic goddess of inspiration and debauchery
Cf: Persephone (Greek)

What Windows This?

The antlered dancer chants a vision
Wilderness surrounds, in moist welcome
Inner angels bedeviled, ritually full
Of fine spirit wine, sap of the forest.

The firelight morphs in and out of crimson
Deer pelts melt in the heat of our fright.
Mates gaze senseless; the swamps' densest frenzy
Overtakes us in the shamaning night.

Hunted and hunter, one with the hunger
We gorge on the source like a huge turbine engine
With circle complete, the dance collapses
Wild and alive in our smiles and our trances.

And All That

> – for Nelson Barquet

Arriving on Man's wings
You instantly adapt.
In knowing tones you bellow
"What is that! What is that!"
Simple animal's random homes
Form your cosmology's bones
Its cornerstone: museum pieces
Manipulation, consumption, and feces.

The Car Wreck

Begin at the beginning.
The tire treads tell a tale
of revolution:
A manufacturered beginning
Gnarled to an entropic ending.
The tall tree arching high behind;
of evolution:
A mixture of disparate elements
Become a continuing compound.
My taut teeth and overbite;
To the future:
Discovered in a mud flat
Inert beneath the ground.

Old Man Ode

I putter about like an old man
Seeking solace in spaces in empty rooms
Understanding in the nothingness.
So much in this world of buying and selling
Leaves me bulimic. I'm sick
But can't finger the source, so I gorge
On the one loneliness I can caress.
Like an elder hugging a pillow
Once shared by someone who cared,
I'm resigned to this life
Of anonymity and indignity.
If I could handle the rough reality
Of the elemental battle, I'd be in the thick of it:
A centurion hurrying this way and that
Lost maps half-committed to my slowly dissipating brain.
But I'm not strong enough to face even
A cashier whose otherness hungrily clutches
The paper I offer for whatever
I decide I need. A friend? A human
Interaction? Some reaction?
No, like an old man in traction
I have broken my hip into squares
That pierce my shin like femur fragments
Abutting this manuscript, rubbed with blood.

It's a Small World, After All

I belong! I belong!
To this brusk, brisk
Brawling, sprawling
Atomic amalgamation
Of brethren beings!
They sing in harmony.
A choir of lyres
Never decorated ancient air
With Lysol scent of today.
The spray of society
Channeled through a plastic knob
Disinfects and deodorizes
The selfish motives
That drove the drops together.
I prefer the rat rot of ancient odor.

Noose

Soon I'll run out of things to say.
Soon I'll run out of things.
Soon I'll run out.
Soon I'll run.
Soon.

Unutterable Blunders and Palace Disasters

I.
Come now this eroding empire
Paradise of products and purchase
Perchance, perhaps, Absurdity
Absolves the hapless inhabitants
For the Irreversible crash.
Come now to a Man, Reasoner,
Thrown in this habitat by happenstance
Battered and bashed
By Lucre's translucent lash.
Hear the myriad gaggle of babble
Gurgling over telephone lines
With origin and destination
Both known and unknown.

II.
Fat white men play you like a computer game.
The numbers governors manufacture
All you are, all you wanted to become,
And what you became.
Tied like a lynch victim
To currency's eternal ephemera
All naught but a chimera
The etched Arabic abstractions
In the N.A.S.D.A.Q. or O.T.C. section
Tabloids void of connection
With origin and destination
Both known and unknown
Fat white men play you like a computer game.
Like mastodon bones they toss
Shadow puppets of fame
For you to chew,
Smog to shroud the palace court
Of each Corporate Park

Executives as monarchs
Managers as feudal lords
The middle class as jesters
Sucking sycophants and peasants
Jockeying to make the Kings laugh
And fatter. Fatter they grow, they bellow
Your moans – A CD of servility
Every note so pure and clear
In this court, you court fear.

III.
With origin and destination
Both known and unknown
You watch T.V.
Without understanding
The electronic components
Of image creation.
You heat your feed
In a microwave
Not comprehending
The physics of radiation.
You fly in planes
Bereft of knowledge
Of the actions and reactions
Within jet turbines.
You flip a light
Not even thinking
Of the tools and fuels
Molding electric sparks.
You live a life
Not knowing why
Cycles of expansion and recession
Tedious toil without redemption
Darkness devoid of emotional expression
Yield only desperation and depression.
In incomprehension you are not alone
Like those thousand million electrons

continued

Coded voices through phone lines
You are in the mainstream
Yet only one at a time can you scream.
For every Transco Tower, there is toxic waste
For every Chartes Cathedral, there is a fart
With origin and destination
Both known and unknown
Your moments are suspended in slo-mo.

IV.
You, Reasoner, you are alone
A Thinker on a throne
In a pose of waste disposal.
You, Reasoner, Man whose sons and daughters
Like you will willfully consent to the slaughter
Of spirit for the benefit
Of recycling spit and shit.
You fought for naught
But the dense settled sense
Of questions answered
In cosmological somersaults
Still yielding unanswerable bottoms.
The hollow of your soul
And the world blew you apart
Like a 20-megaton explosion
The light blinding
The blastwave devastating
Any and all ground
You thought you found
To stand firm on
With origin and destination
Both known and unknown
You, Reasoner, are a criminal, artificial
Creation desiring imposition
On the hollow null set
You and your fellows inhabit
This is it and you know this is it
And you know nothing and nothing will change it.

About the Author

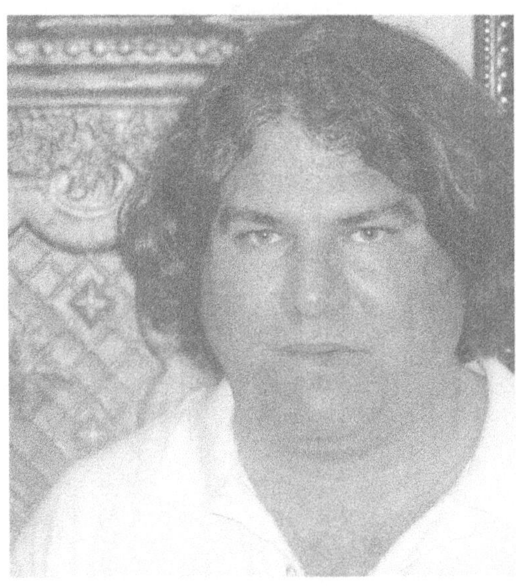

Ken Jones has been a published poet for over 20 years in academic and underground journals, magazines, anthologies, websites and other forums. He earned his M.A. in English/Creative Writing from The University of Texas at Austin and is a full-time faculty member at The Art Institute of Houston where he teaches Creative Writing, among other subjects. Jones also recorded and performed as a poet/musician in Austin and Los Angeles in the 1980's and 1990's and is a licensed attorney in the state of Texas with a J.D. from the University of Southern California.